The Walking With God Series

The Incomparable Jesus
Experiencing the Power of Christ

Don Cousins & Judson Poling

Zondervan Publishing House
Grand Rapids, Michigan

A Division of HarperCollinsPublishers

The Walking With God Series

Friendship With God:
Developing Intimacy With God

The Incomparable Jesus:
Experiencing the Power of Christ

"Follow Me!":
Walking With Jesus in Everyday Life

Discovering the Church:
Becoming Part of God's New Community

Building Your Church:
Using Your Gifts, Time, and Resources

Impacting Your World:
Becoming a Person of Influence

Published by Zondervan Publishing House, Grand Rapids, Michigan 49530

Produced by The Livingstone Corporation. James C. Galvin, J. Michael Kendrick, Daryl J. Lucas, and Darcy J. Kamps, project staff.

ISBN 0-310-59153-8

Cover design: Mark Veldheer
Interior design: Catherine Bergstrom

Printed in the United States of America
95 96 97 98 99 / DP / 9 8 7

Preface

The *Walking With God Series* was developed as the curriculum for small groups at Willow Creek Community Church in South Barrington, Illinois. This innovative church has grown to over 15,000 in less than two decades, and the material here flows out of the vision and values of this dynamic ministry. Groups using these studies have produced many of the leaders, both staff and volunteer, throughout the church.

Associate Pastor Don Cousins wrote the first draft of this material and used it with his own small group. After testing it there, he revised it and passed his notes to Judson Poling, Director of Curriculum Development, who edited and expanded the outlines. Several pilot groups helped shape the material as it was being written and revised. A team of leaders labored through a line-by-line revision of these study guides over a year's span of time. Finally, these revisions were put into this new, more usable format.

Any church or group can use these studies in a relational context to help raise up devoted disciples. Group members who finish all six books will lay a solid foundation for a lifelong walk with God.

Willow Creek Resources is a publishing partnership between Zondervan Publishing House and the Willow Creek Association. Willow Creek Resources will include drama sketches, small group curricula, training material, videos, and many other specialized ministry resources.

Willow Creek Association is an international network of churches ministering to the unchurched. Founded in 1992, the Willow Creek Association serves churches through conferences, seminars, regional roundtables, consulting, and ministry resource materials. The mission of the Association is to assist churches in reestablishing the priority and practice of reaching lost people for Christ through church ministries targeted to seekers.

For conference and seminar information please write to:

Willow Creek Association
P.O. Box 3188
Barrington, Illinois 60011-3188

Contents

The Incomparable Jesus

Experiencing the Power of Christ

Introduction

What do you do well? Most of us have some skill or distinguishing trait for which we're recognized. One person can work with cars, another person is knowledgeable about history, someone else has a great sense of humor. Some people are known for what they make, some for how they serve, some for what they do, others for what they say. God made us all different, and that differentness is shown in the gifts we bring to the rest of the world as we fulfill the potential vested in each of us by our creative Creator. We're able to become proficient as we cultivate, practice, and focus on those skills or areas of interest. Whatever captivates our minds and hearts—whatever becomes second-nature to us—eventually forms how we're perceived by the world around us. We become someone special to others by having something special to offer—all of which flows from being attracted to and spending time absorbed in a special area of interest.

What do you do well that you can offer in service to God? Is there anything you're known for that relates to eternal concerns? What has captivated your mind and heart—what has become second nature—that you can present to your world in a unique and purposeful way in the name of Jesus? The shared goal of every Christian, no matter how we're wired individually, is to become like Jesus. We will each have a unique gift to offer that will make us different, but we will all be striving for the same qualities when we strive after Christian character. We don't all need to be experts at the same thing—in fact, God designed the church, as we'll see in later books in this series, so that nobody would be an island of competence. But everyone who names the name of Christ must do as Christ did, and that can only happen as we become "experts" at knowing Jesus. Details of theology may seem tedious or even boring, but none of us should yawn when we say, "Jesus is Lord" and try to understand what that means. Others may spend hours drawing prophecy charts, but every one of us must draw on the power and wisdom of the One whose future reign over all is certain. We all have different "minors," but every believer must major on Jesus.

This study guide covers the preparations God made to send his Son into the world, and continues with discussions of the means and meat of his message. It is really the first of a two-part study on the life of Jesus completed in the next book in the *Walking with God Series*, "Follow Me!" Through these pages you'll discover anew the Messiah of Scripture and perhaps even revise some of your views of him. You'll take important steps toward a more accurate—and stronger—connection with the incomparable Jesus.

They Said He's Coming—The Prophecies

Many Christians don't appreciate or understand the vital connection between the Old Testament and the New Testament. For example, there are over 300 prophecies in the Old Testament that refer specifically to the life of Christ! All of these prophecies came about just as predicted. This is especially amazing when you consider that more than 20 different authors wrote them over a 1,000-year period.

The probability of one person fulfilling just eight of the Old Testament prophecies is one in 10 to the 17th power, or one in 100,000,000,000,000,000 (one hundred million billion). The likelihood of accidentally fulfilling just 48 prophecies is one in 100 to the 157th power. Jesus fulfilled all 300. (See Peter Stoner's book, *Science Speaks,* Moody Press, 1963.)

These prophecies tell us a lot about Jesus. Through the prophets, God revealed many facts about Jesus' birth, life, and death. These signposts not only point to the Savior; they serve as proof of the divine origin of Scripture and confirm the divine nature of Jesus. To begin our study we will look up several prophecies and their fulfillment in the life of Christ.

The Fulfillment of Prophecy

Read these prophecies to see the correlation between them and their fulfillment. Write down how Jesus fulfilled each prophecy.

What was to be unique about Jesus' birth? (Isaiah 7:14 and Matthew 1:18-25)

Where was Jesus to be born? (Micah 5:2 and Matthew 2:1-6)

How would Jesus be honored? (Psalm 72:10-11; Isaiah 60:6; and Matthew 2:11)

Where would Jesus live as a young child? (Hosea 11:1 and Matthew 2:14-15)

How would people be prepared for Jesus' public ministry? (Isaiah 40:3 and Luke 3:3-6)

Where would Jesus minister? (Isaiah 9:1-2 and Matthew 4:12-16)

What amazing feats would Jesus perform? (Isaiah 35:5-6 and Matthew 11:4-5; 15:30-31)

How would Jesus teach? (Psalm 78:2 and Matthew 13:34-35)

How would Jesus be received by others? (Isaiah 53:3 and John 8:48)

For what price would Jesus be betrayed? (Psalm 41:9; Zechariah 11:12-13, and Matthew 27:3-10)

How would Jesus respond to his accusers? (Isaiah 53:7 and Matthew 27:12-14)

How would Jesus die? (Psalm 22:14-18 and Matthew 27:33-44; John 19:17-18, 23-4, 28)

How would Jesus be protected from physical harm? (Psalm 34:20 and John 19:32-36)

What would Jesus' death accomplish? (Isaiah 53:4-6 and 2 Corinthians 5:21)

How would Jesus be buried? (Isaiah 53:9 and Matthew 27:57-60)

What would happen to Jesus' body? (Psalm 16:9-10 and Acts 2:29-32)

The Value of Prophecy

Which of the prophecies about Christ has made the most significant impression on you in this study?

Why is fulfilled prophecy important to Christianity?

How does fulfilled prophecy give you more confidence in God?

BOTTOM LINE

Bible

Set three appointments with God this week. Pick the times during the day that work best for you. Study Matthew 5 three times, noting specific observations and applications.

Prayer

Day One: Adoration—Using Psalm 119, worship God for the trustworthiness of his Word. Then take the chorus to the song, "God Is So Good," and write as many new verses as you can. (For example: God is so fair, God is so kind, God is my friend, He loves us so, I hope in him, and so on.)

Day Two: Confession—Look up Matthew 26:41. Pray for help in an area of frequent temptation in your life.

Day Three: Supplication—Pray for three of your most pressing concerns.

Scripture Memory

As part of the curriculum, we've included memory verses with each study. If you desire to make this discipline part of your discipleship experience, begin by memorizing this verse:

Watch and pray so that you will not fall into temptation. The spirit is willing, but the body is weak. Matthew 26:41

In the next study we will explore the concept that Jesus was both fully God and fully human. To prepare, ask yourself the following questions. Why would Jesus' identity be such a controversial issue that people would kill him over it? If a Christian has the Holy Spirit living inside him, why isn't he considered divine like Jesus? What's the difference?

2

Jesus—The God-man

Think for a moment about a current political figure. What is your opinion of that person? Do other people agree with you? Chances are that every person you meet will have a different perspective. Some will think that he or she is fair-minded, upright, and responsive to the people; others will regard that person as inept, a captive of special interests, or even dangerous!

In much the same way, just about every person has an opinion of Jesus. Many believe he was a great teacher. Some believe he was a humble philosopher whose followers altered then propagated his ideas. Some believe he was our Savior. Some believe he rose from the dead; many do not. A variety of mistaken ideas about who Jesus Christ actually was still float around. As Christians, we have a special responsibility to get a clear and accurate view of Christ. Jesus is at the center of our faith; he—not our moral code, church, or beliefs—is what people reject when they reject Christianity. We are not just "God-ians," but "Christians." What's more, our understanding of Jesus determines how we interact with him, how we respond to him, and—in the end—whether we spend eternity with him. The first step in being true Christians, then, is to understand who Jesus is.

It's important to understand that Jesus is both fully divine and fully human. Throughout church history, heretics have denied one or the other aspect of his nature. This study will help you understand his dual nature and the implications for us.

Jesus' Eternal Existence

What similarities and differences do you observe in Genesis 1:1-3 and John 1:1-3?

What is Jesus' relationship to the creation? (Colossians 1:15-19)

What did Jesus himself claim about his existence? (John 8:58)

When did Jesus share the Father's glory? (John 17:5) Why is this significant

What is the significance of the phrase Jesus used to describe himself in Revelation 1:8, 17 and 22:12-13?

Jesus' Divinity

Even more important than preexistence, the Bible also identifies Jesus as part of the one and only God. He is the second person of the Trinity.

What do you understand the Trinity to mean?

What mistaken ideas do some people have about the Trinity?

What object lesson or illustration have you heard that helps you understand the concept of "Trinity"?

How is Jesus related to God the Father? (John 10:30)

What divine qualities does Jesus have? (Hebrews 1:2-3)

What is Jesus' relationship to the angels? (Hebrews 1:4-6)

What other qualities does Jesus have that belong only to God? (Hebrews 1:8-12)

Jesus' Humanity

In order to come to earth, what was Jesus required to do? (Philippians 2:7-8)

How do we know that Jesus experienced fatigue? (John 4:6)

How do we know that Jesus experienced thirst? (John 4:7)

How do we know that Jesus experienced anger? (John 2:14-17)

How do we know that Jesus had limited knowledge while on earth? (Matthew 24:36)

How do we know that Jesus experienced temptation? (Luke 4:2)

How do we know that Jesus experienced sadness? (John 11:35)

How do we know that Jesus possessed a fully human body? (John 1:14)

The Importance of Jesus' Identity

How does it help us to know that Jesus is fully God? (Hebrews 4:13-14)

How does it help us to know that Jesus was fully human? (Hebrews 4:15-16)

What bearing does our belief about Jesus have on our salvation? (John 8:24)

BOTTOM LINE

YOUR WALK WITH GOD

Bible

Study Matthew 6 three times during your three appointments with God this week and make three observations and specific applications.

Prayer

Day One: Adoration and Thanksgiving—Identify one truth in Matthew 6 for which you can praise and thank God.

Day Two: Confession—Read Hebrews 12:1-4; what do you learn from these verses about your struggle with sin? Review Matthew 26:41 (the memory verse from last week).

Day Three: Supplication—Call one person from the group—make it a surprise—and find out what were his or her three major requests from last week so you can pray for him or her.

Scripture Memory

Your attitude should be the same as that of Christ Jesus: Who, being in very nature God, did not consider equality with God something to be grasped, but made himself nothing, taking the very nature of a servant, being made in human likeness. Philippians 2:5-7

In the next study, we will take a look at the careful preparations that God made for the coming of Christ. To prepare yourself for the discussion, consider the reasons why God would want to be intimately involved even in matters relating to Jesus' birth and family of origin.

Countdown to His Coming

When you were in school, you probably preferred the teachers who showed personal interest in you, ones who called you by your first name and talked with you on a personal level. The ones who simply lectured from the front and didn't connect with you in any way are likely a dim memory for you. We simply don't respond well to a teacher who refuses to enter our personal worlds, no matter how important the lesson he or she may convey to us.

In keeping his promise to send the Messiah, God went far beyond teaching a message; he became personally involved in the lives of individual people. He used a real, live pair of newlyweds named Mary and Joseph to be the parents of his Son, even to the point of sending angels to tell them what would happen and to warn them of dangers. Through these personal visits, he protected and guided them. God did not merely fulfill prophecy himself; he allowed others to participate in the sovereign plan he was unfolding.

This study will show how God prepared the way for Jesus to be born into the world. In this study, you'll see how God's involvement then demonstrates his ongoing desire to be personally involved in our lives today.

The First Promise: John the Baptist

Describe Zechariah and Elizabeth. (Luke 1:5-7)

In your own words describe what happens to Zechariah in Luke 1:8-13.

What do we learn about John the Baptist from this account? (Luke 1:13-17)

How did Zechariah and Elizabeth respond to this good news? (Luke 1:18-25)

What can we learn about our own responses to God from this story?

The Second Promise: Christ Himself

What was the angel's message to Mary? (Luke 1:26-38)

How did Joseph respond to the situation he found himself in? (Matthew 1:18-25)

What are some of the similarities in the circumstances of John the Baptist's and Jesus' births? What are the significant differences?

Do Mary and Joseph's experience provide any lessons for us today?

The Promises Fulfilled

What was the focus of Mary and Elizabeth's conversation? (Luke 1:39-45)

As you read Mary's song of praise, what does she say about God that is just as true today as it was then? (Luke 1:46-56)

What did Mary say about God that especially applies to a need in your life? Describe how that statement could help you.

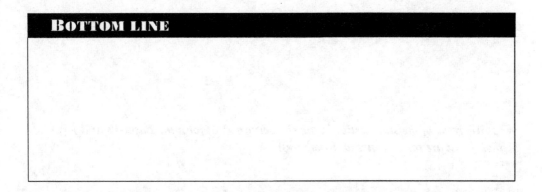

YOUR WALK WITH GOD

Bible

Study Matthew 7 three times, noting observations and applications. Also study the "On Your Own" assignment for background on the four Gospels.

Prayer

Day One: Adoration—Pray using Psalm 113 as a guide.

Day Two: Confession—Review Matthew 26:41, the verse you memorized in the first study of *The Incomparable Jesus.* Jot down a brief log of the last 24 hours: What thoughts, words, or deeds did not please God?

Day Three: Thanksgiving—Make a list of all the circumstances you have going for you. Thank God for each item on your list.

Scripture Memory

In the past God spoke to our forefathers through the prophets at many times and in various ways, but in these last days he has spoken to us by his Son, whom he appointed heir of all things, and through whom he made the universe. **Hebrews 1:1-2**

In the next study we will take a close look at the birth and childhood of Jesus. To prepare, think about the events surrounding the Christmas story. What was remarkable to you about Jesus' birth ?

Background on the Gospels

The first four books in the New Testament tell about the life of Christ. These are complimentary accounts—similar to four newspapers covering the same story, or four books about the same famous person. Each stands alone as an account of the life of Christ, and although they contain many of the same stories and teachings, they were directed to different audiences and written by different authors. Here are some of the similarities and differences between them.

1   Matthew

The Author:

- Was one of the original twelve disciples.
- Also called Levi.
- Mentioned in four lists of the Twelve:

    Matthew 10:3

    Mark 3:18

    Luke 6:15

    Acts 1:13

- Called to follow Jesus.

    Matthew 9:9-13

    Mark 2:14-17

    Luke 5:27-32

- He was a tax collector for the Romans.
- He wrote his Gospel around A.D. 70.

The Book:

Matthew wrote specifically to Jews and emphasized Jesus as king. His purpose was to show the Jews that Jesus fulfilled Old Testament prophecy. He presented Jesus' teaching topically and contrasted Jesus with the Pharisees—Jewish religious experts of the day.

2 Mark

The Author:

- Was a close companion of Peter; told his story through the eyes of Peter.

- Full name was John Mark.

- Was the son of a Mary whose house was a meeting place for the disciples (see Acts 12:12).

- Possibly was converted as a result of Peter's ministry.

- Is mentioned in 2 Timothy 4:11.

- Was a cousin of Barnabas.

- Wrote his Gospel around A.D. 60.

The Book:

Mark wrote mainly to the Romans and emphasized Jesus as servant. Mark recorded Jesus' actions more than his teaching and concentrated on his power and authority.

3 Luke

The Author:

- Mentioned only three times in the New Testament: Colossians 4:14 (called "the beloved physician"), Philemon 24 (Paul's "fellow worker"), and 2 Timothy 4:11 (with Paul right before his death).

- Was a Gentile (non-Jew).

- Was a companion of Paul's on his second and third missionary journeys.

- Wrote his Gospel around A.D. 80.

- Was in Caesarea from A.D. 58 to 60 while Paul was in prison. Since Jerusalem was only a few miles from Caesarea, this would have given him the opportunity to collect firsthand data about Jesus.

The Book:

Luke addressed his Gospel to "Theophilus." It was written to the Greeks, or Gentiles (non-Jews), emphasizing Jesus' humanity. His Gospel is scholarly and historical, dealing with human needs (such as the weak, the suffering, and the outcast) and presents the human side of the Son of God.

4 John

The Author:

- Isn't identified until the end of the book, where he calls himself the "disciple whom Jesus loved" (21:20, 24).

- Father's name was Zebedee (Matthew 4:21).

- Mother seems to have been Salome (Matthew 27:56; Mark 15:40). She may have been the sister of the Mary who was the mother of Jesus. If so, John was Jesus' cousin and could have known him since childhood.

- Was a fisherman.

- Was one of the three inner circle disciples.

- Wrote his Gospel, three epistles, and Revelation.

- Wrote his Gospel around A.D. 90.

The Book:

The Gospel of John is directed at a general audience and emphasizes the deity of Christ. It consists mainly of Jesus' discussions and conversations. John's purpose in writing is spelled out in 20:31: *"These are written that you may believe that Jesus is the Christ, the Son of God, and that by believing you may have life in his name."*

The Early Years

Many people regard the Christmas story as a marvelous, heartwarming event—but one that has little relevance for understanding the life and mission of Jesus while he was on earth. To them, it is mere background or historical detail. What a shame! Because they haven't grasped the tremendous work that God accomplished at Jesus' birth and in his childhood, they often find it difficult to apply this portion of the Gospels to their lives.

But the events surrounding the life of Christ tell us what *happens*, not only what *happened*. The challenge for you is to ask what these events reveal about the character of God. By telling you about what God *did*, they will show you what God does *now*. Though his specific actions may vary throughout history, his character will always be consistent—faithful, powerful, sovereign, caring.

In this study, we will see God's faithfulness in the events that surround the birth and childhood of Jesus.

STUDY

The Birth of John the Baptist

What was the controversy surrounding John's name? (Luke 1:57-66)

What does Zechariah and Elizabeth's insistence on naming their baby John tell us about their character? (Luke 1:13)

What were the results of Zechariah's obedience? (Luke 1:63-67)

What can we learn from this passage that applies to our lives today?

The Birth of Jesus

What additional light did Paul shed on Jesus' birth? (Romans 5:6; Galatians 4:4)

What do we learn from this passage about the kind of man Joseph was? (Matthew 1:19)

What does this passage teach us about the environment that Jesus would be raised in?

How might your response to the angel's announcement of Jesus' birth have been similar to the shepherds' reaction? (Luke 2:8-20)

What was the significance of Mary's reaction to the events surrounding Jesus' birth?
(Luke 2:17-19)

Jesus' Infancy

Why is it significant that Luke includes an account of the child's circumcision? (Luke 2:21)

Why do you think God drew the magi to visit Jesus? (Matthew 2:1-12)

How did Jesus spend his early childhood? (Matthew 2:13-23)

Jesus' Childhood

What kind of religious training did Jesus probably receive? (Deuteronomy 6:4-7)

What do we know about Jesus' later childhood? (Luke 2:39-52)

What do we learn about God and his Son from these details of the early years of Jesus' life?

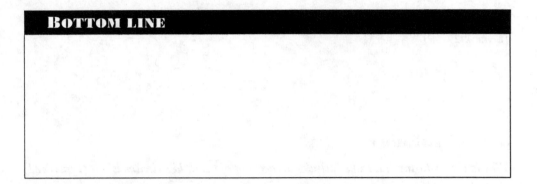

BOTTOM LINE

YOUR WALK WITH GOD

Bible

Study Matthew 8 three times, noting observations and making applications. Also read the material in On Your Own.

Prayer

Day One: Adoration—Identify five specific aspects of creation that point to God's creativity and thank him for them. In order to observe them firsthand, go for a walk and pray as you go.

Day Two: Confession—What progress are you seeing in the area of temptation with which you struggle? To what do you attribute this growth? If there is no progress, why not?

Day Three: Supplication—Write out a prayer about three major concerns in your life. When you are finished, be still for a few moments in God's presence, listening to him. Write down what he is impressing on you.

Scripture Memory

Review Matthew 26:41, Philippians 2:5-7, and Hebrews 1:1-2.

The next study will focus on Satan's temptation of Christ in the wilderness. To prepare, think about the greatest areas of temptation that you face at this time. What do you do to help you resist temptation?

Who was John the Baptist?

One of the most colorful characters in the New Testament is John the Baptist. John lived in the wilderness under rugged conditions. His appearance was striking, even strange. We read that his clothes were made of camel's hair and that he ate locusts and wild honey. But John made God's righteousness a public issue. His message could be summed up by the theme "repent and live righteously." He challenged those secure in their religious attitudes to abandon their sin or face judgment. By doing so he prepared the way for the One who would embody righteousness and deliver those who turned to God from that coming judgment.

John the Baptist was certainly an unusual person, but his life and message had a very positive effect on the people of his day—he took a stand, he was a man of convictions, he promised new life through repentance, he lived continuously filled with God's Spirit. These and other qualities made him highly esteemed by the masses. Just as John the Baptist paved the way for the Messiah on earth back then, the account of his life and actions can make a highway to prepare you for the work of Jesus in your life today.

There is a fine line between the truth that attracts and differences that repel! For many Christians, being different means being odd. Some will "major on minors"—in other words, they mark themselves by what they don't do: no smoking, no drinking, no card playing, and so on. Such behavior, however, isn't necessarily an indication of true spirituality. It is far better to develop an internal character that stands out. The watching world may then come to say "Christians are people who are compassionate and generous, who serve others and who are role models for upright living." They will say "Christians *are*" rather than "Christians *don't*."

What about you? Do people perceive you as different? In an attractive way? Remember that the kind of difference that brings people to God is found in the lives of servants like John the Baptist.

Who Were the Wise Men?

The wise men were students of the stars, or astrologers, who probably came from Persia (modern-day Iran). Because the Jews were one time under Persian rule, the Persians were probably familiar with the religion of the Jews and their Messianic hopes.

In seeking out the new born king, their first stop was not Bethlehem, but Jerusalem. They checked in with Herod, naively assuming he and his court would be excited about the Messiah. They were excited—but not in the way the wise men assumed. Insecure and treacherous, Herod planned to kill the child and eliminate a future rival. He asked the wise men to report back to him when they had found the Christ child so that he could "worship" too. But these men were warned in a dream not to go back to Herod and returned to their country via a different route.

Even though they were not Jews, the wise men were quick to realize the majesty and significance of Jesus' birth. They presented him valuable treasures and worshipped him. Their arrival was a foreshadowing of the good news that would soon be available to all people, regardless or race or culture, who trusted in Christ for salvation.

Who Was Herod?

Herod was given the title of king of the Jews by the Romans, but his title was never accepted by the people. He was consumed by worries over his own position and power. He had ten wives over the years, two of whom he had killed. He killed three of his own sons, plus his brother-in-law and one of his wife's grandfathers. The news about the baby born to be king threatened his already shaky security. Knowing this about his nature and character helps us to understand why he ordered that all baby boys under the age of two be killed.

The Temptation of Jesus

We all struggle with temptation. The specific temptations each of us faces differs from person to person, but none of us escapes all of them. And whether or not we ask God to save us from it, it always returns. We seem never to be done with our evil desires.

What can we do about temptation? Centuries ago Martin Luther said, "You cannot keep birds from flying over your head, but you can keep them from building a nest in your hair!" Temptations, like birds in the air, will always be with us. But we should not, nor do we have to, allow them to "roost." We can resist.

Jesus faced temptation countless times. We can learn a great deal about how to resist from the way he resisted. We have one story of temptation he resisted just before his public ministry began. After fasting for forty days, the devil came personally and presented three temptations aimed right at Jesus' human weaknesses. The way Jesus resisted can teach us how to keep sin from "roosting" in our lives.

The First Temptation

Read Matthew 4:1-11.

Describe the circumstances surrounding Jesus' time of temptation. (Matthew 3:13-17)

What did Satan first tempt Jesus to do? (Matthew 4:3-4)

What would be tempting about suggesting that Jesus miraculously make bread?

Why would it have been wrong for Jesus to give in to Satan's temptation?

How did Jesus respond? (Matthew 4:4)

How can we imitate Jesus' example of resisting temptation here?

The Second Temptation

What was the second temptation Jesus faced? (Matthew 4:5-7)

Why would it have been wrong for Jesus to give in to Satan's temptation?

How did Jesus respond? (Matthew 4:7)

The Third Temptation

What was the third temptation Satan tried on Jesus? (Matthew 4:8-10)

What was the significance of this temptation?

How did Jesus respond? (Matthew 4:10)

What We Can Learn

What do we learn about Satan's tactics from this story?

What can we learn about resisting temptation from Jesus' example?

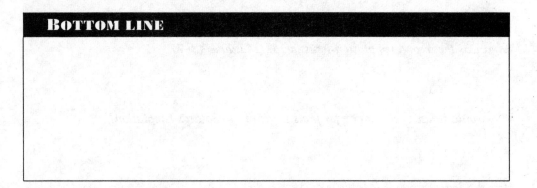

Bible

Study Matthew 9 and 10 at least two times on each chapter.

Prayer

Day One: Adoration—Make a list of answers to this question: How has God shown his love for you recently? Praise God for each one.

Day Two: Confession—Paraphrase Psalm 51:1-4, putting it in words that speak directly to you, and use it as a guide for your prayer.

Day Three: Thanksgiving—Use Psalm 136 as a guide for your prayer.

Scripture Memory

No temptation has seized you except what is common to man. And God is faithful; he will not let you be tempted beyond what you can bear. But when you are tempted, he will also provide a way out so that you can stand up under it.   1 Corinthians 10:13

Next, we will take a look at the message of salvation that Jesus brought to the world. To prepare for the study, summarize in your own words what you would consider the main message of Jesus to be.

The Message Jesus Brought

It was many years ago, but you're sure you could get there again if you had to. You went to that quaint little restaurant on your honeymoon—how could you forget? And now you've just told a friend who's visiting the same area to be sure to go there. You've given him directions, confident your recollections accurately describe the way to get to the best seafood in town. Confident, that is, until you get a call from your friend because the roads don't go the way you recollected, and he went 45 minutes out of his way trusting in the map you drew from your memory. You hang up the phone wondering how you could have been so certain when you were so certainly wrong.

Many people think they have the facts straight about the Gospels and the identity of Jesus, but when they actually delve into message of the New Testament, they realize that several of their cherished ideas need serious revision. In the Gospel of John we encounter one such man who thought he understood God's ways but had to encounter the reality of his erroneous thinking. Nicodemus was not an atheist, but a religious teacher—someone familiar with God's revelation. In some ways, he was like many people today who are religious but misinformed—people who need the new birth from heaven brought by the Spirit. Jesus' statements to Nicodemus put the gospel message—the basic message of salvation—into a clear, concise package. We too should turn to this story as a model of how the gospel should be shared with others.

Jesus' Talk with Nicodemus

What do we know about Nicodemus? (John 3:1-2)

How do we know that Nicodemus respected Jesus? (John 3:2)

How did Jesus answer Nicodemus' words? (John 3:3)

What did Nicodemus misunderstand about Jesus' saying, "You must be born again"? (John 3:4)

Jesus' Talk with the Woman at the Well

What kind of person did Jesus meet? (John 4:4-8, 17-18)

How did Jesus answer the woman's question? (John 4:9-10)

What did Jesus want the woman to understand? (John 4:10-14, 25-26)

Jesus' Main Message

How would you summarize Jesus' main message? (John 3:16; John 4:13-14)

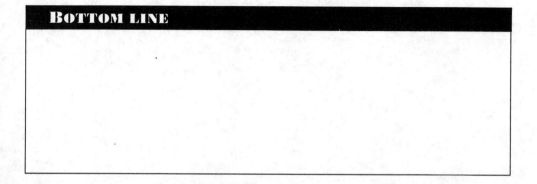

BOTTOM LINE

YOUR WALK WITH GOD

Bible

Study Matthew 11 three times, noting observations and applications.

Prayer

Day One: Adoration—How has God shown his patience to you recently? Thank him for his patience.

Day Two: Confession—Paraphrase Psalm 51:5-9 as you did with verses 1-4, and pray through it.

Day Three: Supplication—What are the three greatest needs in your life right now? Pray about those needs.

Scripture Memory

For God so loved the world that he gave his one and only Son, that whoever believes in him shall not perish but have eternal life.   John 3:16

Next week we will study about those who followed Jesus—the disciples. What did Jesus want his disciples to be? What do you think Jesus expects out of a disciple today?

Jesus Selects His Team

The starting gun goes off. The crowd of runners surges forward. The spectators cheer. The TV cameras record the early leaders and the sports commentators tell us about those who have begun well.

But this is a *marathon*, not a sprint. Once the initial excitement of the start wears off, we become distracted by something else. Later in the day we'll turn back to see who wins. Only at the finish line will the thrill of the start be matched—and exceeded. What happens in between is usually of little interest to the spectators, yet that is where the race is won or lost.

The Christian life is like a marathon. Many enter and even start well. But it's hard to tell who's going to hang in there. Some get distracted or lack the endurance to finish. Others are deceived by their own confidence, tripping because they aren't cautious. Those who finish the race have disciplined their minds and bodies. They aren't sprinters, but long-distance runners. When the tedium and pain of the mid-race are almost unbearable, they persevere. They are the ones who finish well.

Jesus called the apostles to a marathon that we also know as discipleship. Some of them started well. Some of them tripped up along the way. One left the race—never to enter again. But Jesus wanted all of them to follow him—for the long haul.

The purpose of this study is to learn from the experience of the disciples that Jesus wants us to follow him for life.

Jesus' Disciples Then

What considerations did Jesus likely weigh when selecting the twelve apostles? (Luke 6:12-16)

Why is it significant that Jesus called the apostles to "be with him"? (Mark 3:14)

What happened to this group of twelve apostles by the time Jesus left earth? (Acts 1:21-26)

Jesus' Disciples Today

What initially attracted you to Jesus–why did you become a Christian?

Why do you still follow Jesus?

Some disciples of Jesus stopped following him after a while (John 6:66-71). What causes Christians to give up following Christ?

What are some of the benefits of staying faithful to Christ?

What motivates you to stay faithful to Jesus?

What do you need to do to be a better disciple?

YOUR WALK WITH GOD

Bible

Study Matthew 12:1-21 three times, noting observations and applications.

Prayer

Day One: Adoration—How has God shown his grace (undeserved favor) to you recently? Thank him for his grace.

Day Two: Confession—Paraphrase Psalm 51:10-13 so that it reflects you and your circumstances, and use it as a guide for your prayer.

Day Three: Supplication—Identify some specific answers to prayer, as well as taking up some new requests.

Scripture Memory

Do you not know that in a race all the runners run, but only one gets the prize? Run in such a way as to get the prize.   1 Corinthians 9:24

To prepare for the next study, write down a wise saying or quote that provided direction or comfort in your life at some point.

The NewAttitudes

What would you do if you were turned down for a lucrative job after weeks of grueling interviews? Would you sit back, become depressed, and blame yourself for not being a more dynamic person? Or would you take the setback in stride and look forward to the next opportunity? It all depends on your *attitude.* The attitudes that shape our actions often go a long way in determining the quality of our friendships, the performance of our jobs, and our service for God. In a very real way, attitude is everything.

Attitude is the central theme of one of the most famous passages in all of Scripture: the Sermon on the Mount found in Matthew 5—7. The Sermon on the Mount is central to Jesus' teaching, summarizing the characteristics of those who know God personally. Here Jesus instructs us on how we ought to live and who we ought to be. It is a message Jesus gave repeatedly as he traveled from place to place.

This is the first of two studies on the Sermon on the Mount. This study covers Matthew 5:1-16, the section in which Jesus describes believers' NewAttitudes or "Beatitudes," as they're often called. We will learn several ways in which Jesus wants our attitudes and actions to be different from the world's.

The Beatitudes

What does it mean to be poor in spirit? (Matthew 5:3)

What should we mourn over? (Matthew 5:4)

What does it mean to be meek? (Matthew 5:5)

Why is it important for us to desire righteousness? (Matthew 5:6)

Why is it important to show mercy to others? (Matthew 5:7)

What is purity in heart? (Matthew 5:8)

What does it mean to be a "peacemaker"? (Matthew 5:9)

Why are righteous people sometimes persecuted? (Matthew 5:10-12)

The Beatitudes vs. the World's Attitudes

Fill in the blanks from your experience:

Jesus Says	The World Says
Blessed are the poor in spirit	_____
Blessed are those who mourn	_____
Blessed are the meek	_____
Blessed are those who hunger and thirst for righteousness	_____
Blessed are the merciful	_____
Blessed are the pure in heart	_____
Blessed are the peacemakers	_____
Blessed are those who are persecuted because of righteousness	_____

Which of these attitudes do you find most difficult to live out? Why?

Knowing that Jesus wants you to display eventually all of these attitudes, where do you think he would want you to start this week?

What steps can you take to live out these NewAttitudes?

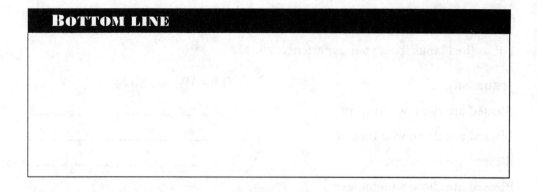

YOUR WALK WITH GOD

Bible

Study Matthew 12:22-50 during your three appointments with God.

Prayer

Day One: Adoration—In what recent situation have you clearly seen God's wisdom?

Day Two: Confession—Paraphrase Psalm 51:14-19, applying it to your own struggle with sin, and use it as a guide for prayer.

Day Three: Thanksgiving—List five things related to your family for which you are thankful.

Scripture Memory

Review the following verses: 1 Corinthians 10:13; John 3:16; and 1 Corinthians 9:24.

Next week we will continue our study of the Sermon on the Mount. Take some time to consider your motives for your behavior? Why is it so difficult to have pure motives?

The Power of Pure Motives

It is easy to judge people by what you see. Want to know who's the most committed to the church? Just look at who arrives on Sunday morning first and stays the longest. Want to know who reads God's Word faithfully? Just look at the person who brings a well-worn Bible to small group. It is tempting to measure each other by what we see outwardly. It is also easy to judge motives unfairly. In particular, we tend to believe that our motives are pure and suspect the motives of others.

God is as concerned with your motives as he is with your outward behavior. He cares about why and how you give, not just how much. He is concerned with why you do good, not just that you do it. Outward obedience alone does not impress God. He wants your heart. In this study, you will explore the importance of your motives in all you do.

STUDY

The Power of Pure Motives

How do inner attitudes and thoughts affect our outward behavior?

Why is it difficult to do good deeds in secret?

Motives to Watch

1 Murder

What inner feelings or attitudes are identified with the outward behavior of murder? (Matthew 5:21-26)

2 Adultery

Why did Jesus go beyond condemning the act of adultery? (Matthew 5:27-28)

Why do you think Jesus used such violent imagery to describe how we should resist sin? (Matthew 5:29-30)

3 Hatred

What inner attitude toward enemies did Jesus condemn? (Matthew 5:43-44)

How do we combat the tendency to scorn our enemies? (Matthew 5:43-44)

4 Giving

What do we need to watch out for in doing good? (Matthew 6:1)

How should we give? (Matthew 6:2-4)

5 Praying

How would you describe prayer that is pleasing to God? (Matthew 6:5-8)

6 Fasting

In what way should we fast? (Matthew 6:16-18)

7 Storing up Treasures

What is a spiritual attitude toward material things?

8 Worry

Why is it harmful to worry about having enough material things? (Matthew 6:25-34)

As you look over this study, what motives do you recognize that hinder your relationship with God? (Matthew 6:25-34)

What steps could you take to bring your inner self more in line with God's desire for you?

BOTTOM LINE

YOUR WALK WITH GOD

Bible

Study Matthew 13 three times. Focus on the Parable of the Seeds.

Prayer

Day One: Adoration—Go for a walk. Carry on a simple conversation with God that includes elements of adoration, confession, thanksgiving, and supplication. Try talking softly out loud as you walk.

Day Two: Supplication—Say something or do something to encourage someone else. You could write a note, make a phone call, buy a small gift, or make something. Then pray specifically for that person.

Day Three: Confession—Take an inventory of your life. Claim God's forgiveness for any sin you recall. Also respond to the following two questions:

- What do you need God's power for this week?

- What do you need God's wisdom for this week?

Scripture Memory

But the LORD said to Samuel, "Do not consider his appearance or his height, for I have rejected him. The LORD does not look at the things man looks at. Man looks at the outward appearance, but the LORD looks at the heart."   1 Samuel 16:7

Next week we will explore some of the parables that Jesus spoke. Why do you think Jesus told so many parables when he could have simply explained the principles he wanted to communicate?

He Spoke in Parables

A mother sits in a rocking chair, holding a child in her lap and a book so that the child can see. As she reads, the child listens in rapt attention. Perhaps you remember having stories read to you. If so, you can probably also remember many details of the stories you heard. Stories have a way of sticking with us over the years.

Pastors also always use stories in the form of illustrations in their sermons. You probably can remember a story your pastor told last week more readily than you can remember his main points. That's because our minds retain pictures more easily than words.

Jesus told many stories. He took common, ordinary experiences and used them to explain spiritual truths that he wanted his disciples to put into practice. We call these stories parables. Altogether the Gospels contain 32 different parables. This is an important part of what Jesus taught. If we are to learn from Jesus, we must become students of his parables.

This study highlights eight of Jesus' parables, all from Matthew 13. You will examine them closely to learn how to learn from a parable.

STUDY

The Sower and the Seed

What is the main point of this parable? (Matthew 13:1-23)

61

Was there a time in your life when your "soil" was not ready to receive God's Word?

The Tares among the Wheat

What lesson did Jesus want to communicate in comparing people to tares and wheat? (Matthew 13:24-30, 36-43)

The Mustard Seed

Why did Jesus choose the mustard seed to illustrate faith? (Matthew 13:31-32)

The Leaven

What qualities does yeast possess that would make it a fitting illustration of the kingdom of heaven? (Matthew 13:33)

The Hidden Treasure

What is the main point of this parable? (Matthew 13:44)

The Costly Pearl

Why is a pearl of great value like the kingdom of heaven? (Matthew 13:45-46)

The Fishing Net

Why would Jesus compare a fishing net to the kingdom of heaven? (Matthew 13:47-50)

The Unmerciful Servant

What is the main point of this parable? (Matthew 18:21-35)

Why do you think Jesus used so many parables in his teaching? (Matthew 13:1-23)

Which of the above parables relates to a concern you have for someone else? Explain your answer.

BOTTOM LINE

Bible

Read Matthew 14 three times, noting observations and applications.

Prayer

Day One: Adoration—Listen to one side of a praise tape in an undistracted, quiet atmosphere.

Day Two: Confession—Call someone in the group and ask him or her to pray for you concerning a temptation you face. Pray together on the phone or at some other time.

Day Three: Supplication—Pray specifically for one aspect of the ministry of your church.

Scripture Memory

But seek first his kingdom and his righteousness, and all these things will be given to you as well.   Matthew 6:33

Next week we will take a closer look at the compassion that Jesus demonstrated for people. Why do some people think that God lacks compassion?

Jesus — A Man of Compassion

PURPOSE

"You say that God loves the world, but I don't feel it."

"God is out there and I am here, what does it mean to say I matter to him?"

"Jesus could never love me after the things I've done."

Most people have trouble feeling God's love. Some just don't feel much of anything, so God's love seems meaningless to them. Some are pressed down under the weight of their failures and feel too ashamed and unworthy to embrace God's care. It's difficult to grow in a relationship with God without becoming aware of and accepting his compassion for us. Yet when we understand the depth of God's great tenderness toward us, we are better able to love him back in response.

The purpose of this study is to help you understand the compassionate side of Jesus. You'll learn that Jesus wants to show compassion to those in need—including you.

STUDY

Jesus and the Death of Lazarus

What was Jesus' response to the news of Lazarus' death? (John 11:33-38)

Can you relate to Jesus' feelings here?

What does this tell you about Jesus?

Jesus and the Multitudes

What does Jesus' response to the death of John the Baptist tell you about how he was feeling?

When Jesus saw the large crowd that had gathered to see him, how did he view the interruption on his attempt to get away? (Matthew 14:13-14)

How would you describe the disciples' attitude toward the crowd? (Matthew 14:15)

Jesus and You

Tell about a time that someone showed compassion toward you. What kind of impact did this have on you?

Read Matthew 11:28-30. What is one way Jesus demonstrate his compassion? Explain how this compassion is manifested practically in a Christian's life.

What makes it easy or difficult for you to see Jesus as compassionate?

In what way has Jesus' compassion touched your life in a way you can feel?

Jesus and Your World

Why do people sometimes find it hard to believe that God loves them?

In what settings are you able to share Christ's compassion with others?

What can you do this week to show Christ's compassion to another person in need?

BOTTOM LINE

Bible

Read Matthew 15 three times, noting observations and applications.

Prayer

Day One: Adoration—List attributes of God that you think of easily when observing or enjoying creation.

Day Two: Confession—Go for a walk and use it as a time to "clear the air" between you and the Lord. Be thorough, and claim his complete forgiveness.

Day Three: Thanksgiving—Fill in the following blanks, thanking God for . . .

A spiritual blessing: _____

A friendship blessing: _____

A family blessing: _____

A spouse or relational blessing: _____

A material blessing: _____

Scripture Memory

Come to me, all you who are weary and burdened, and I will give you rest. Matthew 11:28

Next week we will take a closer look at the times when Jesus healed those who were sick. What difference do you think it made that Jesus could heal those who were sick? Do you think God still heals people in our day?

Jesus the Healer

If you moved to a new city, how would you choose your family physician? Chances are you would take into consideration a number of important qualifications. Certainly you would want someone who was knowledgeable and who kept up with the rapid changes in medicine. Just as important, however, would be that doctor's concern for your entire well being. You would want to sense that this physician genuinely cared about *you* and would want to do everything in his or her power to keep you well or help you get over an illness.

Jesus' healing ministry was a highly personal part of his work. Lest we imagine huge crowds gathered to watch him perform these great miracles, we should keep in mind that he taught the masses, but healed individuals. Even when others were looking, he performed healings by touching each person one by one. (The only exception was when he healed ten lepers as a group, but even then they were apart from the crowd.) Remember that one of Satan's temptations was to lure Jesus into using his power to razzle-dazzle potential followers (Matthew 4:5-6). Jesus did not use his healing power to draw crowds. He healed people to substantiate his claims and to demonstrate his compassion. He wanted people to be healed, and he also wanted them to understand that he was the one they were waiting for—the Messiah.

This study will show you that Jesus did indeed heal those who were sick. You can have confidence in his compassion and his power to help you in times of need.

Healing the Centurion's Servant

What facts do you observe about the centurion? (Luke 7:1-10)

What can this story teach us about asking Jesus to heal others? (Luke 7:1-10)

Raising the Widow's Son

What strikes you about the healing of the widow's son? (Luke 7:11-17)

What does this story teach us about Jesus?

Raising Jairus' Daughter

Who was Jairus? (Mark 5:21-43)

What can this story teach us about trusting God?

Healing of the Hemorrhaging Woman

What impresses you about the woman Jesus healed? (Mark 5:24-34)

What can this story teach us about asking Jesus for help?

Healing of Ten Lepers

What are some significant details in this healing? (Luke 17:11-19)

What can this story teach us about expecting to see results from our prayers?

Conclusion

What general observation can you make from the healings studied here?

What do these healings show us about the nature of Jesus?

How do we know it's worthwhile to pray about physical and emotional needs in our life?

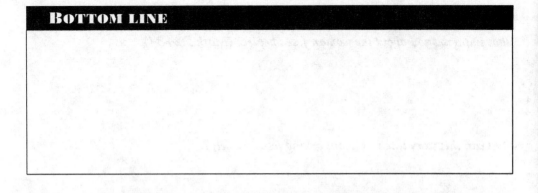

YOUR WALK WITH GOD

Bible

Read Psalm 23 three times. Also, review the application questions in On Your Own.

Prayer

Day One: Adoration—Write down your thoughts to this question: What does the sending of Jesus tell you about God? Spend some time praising him for what you found.

Day Two: Confession—Think back over the events and conversations of this week. For what do you need to claim God's forgiveness?

Day Three: Thanksgiving—List three positive values you picked up from your family. Thank God for them, and then tell your parents or your siblings your thoughts if possible.

Scripture Memory

Review the following verses: 1 Samuel 16:7; Matthew 6:33; and Matthew 11:28.

Next week we will review the main lessons learned in *The Incomparable Jesus*. What have you learned about Jesus? What other insights have been helpful?

Questions for Application

One reason why some Christians find Bible study lifeless and routine is that they fail to apply the passages they've read to their lives. Many times the solution to this problem is to develop a regular habit of asking questions that will help you personalize the Scripture message you've read. We've drawn up a list of questions you can use. Try them this week as you are reading your Bible assignment.

Is there a promise to claim?

Is there a command to obey?

Is there sin to confess?

Is there an example to follow?

Is there a behavior to change?

Is there an encouragement to receive?

Is there an insight to gain?

Is there an issue to pray about?

Is there a reason to worship God?

Reviewing The Incomparable Jesus

This review culminates your study of *The Incomparable Jesus,* the second book in the *Walking With God Series.* Use this time to reflect on your experience and summarize what you've learned about Christ. It can also be an affirming time to express your appreciation to fellow group members for the growing bond between you.

Being a Christian means more than just knowing about Jesus; it means knowing him personally. Our knowledge of Christ should change us. As you do this review, spend time sharing how Jesus is changing you.

Discoveries about Jesus

Why is it significant that Jesus fulfilled the prophecies of the Old Testament?

Why is it important to affirm that Jesus was both fully God and fully man?

What do we learn about resisting temptation from Jesus resisting Satan in the wilderness?

What do we learn about ministering to others from the way Jesus selected and nurtured his twelve apostles?

How would you summarize Jesus' main message (the gospel)?

Which of the Beatitudes do you find to be the most challenging to apply?

Why does religious behavior without the proper motives fail to please God?

How do we know that Jesus has compassion on us?

What are some biblical examples of Jesus showing concern for individual people?

Discoveries about Yourself

During the past twelve weeks, how have you grown in your relationship with Jesus?

Name two or three specific ways you are trying to be different as a result of this study.

In what ways has this study of the incomparable Jesus affected your attitudes?

BOTTOM LINE

YOUR WALK WITH GOD

Bible

You are free to study any passage, chapter, or book of the Bible this week, but be prepared to discuss any observations or applications you noted.

Prayer

Pray that you'll come to know Christ more deeply.

Scripture Memory

Review the following verses: Matthew 26:41; Philippians 2:5-7; Hebrews 1:1-2; 1 Corinthians 10:13; John 3:16; 1 Corinthians 9:24; 1 Samuel 16:7; Matthew 6:33; Matthew 11:28.

ON YOUR OWN

Self-Evaluation

Your group leader will be meeting with you to discuss your current spiritual condition and your hopes for growing in your faith. Please take some time to reflect honestly on where you stand right now within these four basic categories of Christian growth. Rate yourself in each category.

+ **Doing well. I'm pleased with my progress so far.**

✓ **On the right track, but I see definite areas for improvement.**

- **This is a struggle. I need some help.**

A Disciple Is One Who . . .

Walks with God

To what extent is my Bible study and prayer time adequate for helping me walk with God?

Rating:

Comments:

Lives the Word

To what extent is my mind filled with scriptural truths so that my actions and reactions show I am being transformed?

Rating:

Comments:

Contributes to the work

To what extent am I actively participating in the church with my time, talents, and treasures?

Rating:

Comments:

Impacts the world

To what extent am I impacting my world with a Christian witness and influence?

Rating:

Comments:

Other issues I would like to discuss with my small group leader:

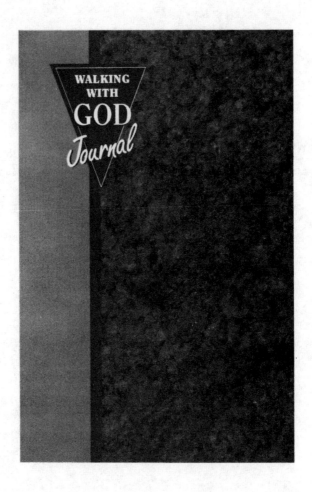

The *Walking With God Journal* is the perfect companion to the *Walking With God Series*. Use it to keep your notes during Bible study, record your prayers, or simply jot down your thoughts and insights. (0-310-91642-9)

NOTES

NOTES